EYE TO EYE WITH DOGS

LABRADOODLES

Lynn M. Stone

Rourke
Publishing LLC
Vero Beach, Florida 32964

CHILDREN'S LIBRARY

www.rourkepublishing.com

PHOTO CREDITS: All photos © Lynn M. Stone

Editor: Meg Greve

Cover and page design by Nicola Stratford

Library of Congress Cataloging-in-Publication Data

Stone, Lynn M.
  Labradoodles / Lynn M. Stone.
    p. cm. -- (Eye to eye with dogs)
  Includes index.
  ISBN 978-1-60472-363-2
  1. Labradoodle--Juvenile literature. I. Title.
  SF429.L29S76 2009
  636.72--dc22
                                2008012977

Printed in the USA

CG/CG

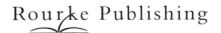

Rourke Publishing

www.rourkepublishing.com – rourke@rourkepublishing.com
Post Office Box 3328, Vero Beach, FL 32964

Table of Contents

The Labradoodle 5

Looks 11

Labradoodles of the Past 13

The Dog for You? 18

A Note about Dogs 22

Glossary 23

Index 24

The Australian Labradoodle is a handsome dog with a winning personality.

The Labradoodle

The Australian Labradoodle is a newcomer to the dog world, but it is already popular.

The Labradoodle is a mix of the Labrador retriever and standard poodle. People choose the Australian Labradoodle as a pet, **guide dog**, or **therapy** companion. Guide dogs receive special training to lead blind people.

AUSTRALIAN LABRADOODLE FACTS

Weight: 45 to 75 pounds (20 to 34 kilograms)
Height: 21 to 24 inches (54 to 62 centimeters)
Country of Origin: Australia
Life Span: 13 to 15 years

Therapy dogs are patient, good-natured dogs. Trained to be companions, Australian Labradoodles work in schools, hospitals, and homes for elderly people.

Some consider the Australian Labradoodle to be a pure **breed**, or **purebred**, already, like a golden retriever or Yorkshire terrier. However, it will take some years before the Australian Labradoodle is a true purebred.

The Labradoodle began as a cross between a Labrador retriever and a standard poodle.

Purebred parents of the same breed usually produce pups very much like the parents themselves. Their pups typically grow to be similar in size, shape, and **temperament** to the parents.

These Chesapeake retriever pups will grow up to look like their purebred parents.

Not all Labradoodles have predictable pups. Some Labradoodles, for example, might shed much more than others, even if they have the same parents.

For now, many Labradoodle **breeders** are still experimenting with the mix. Some breeders cross one type of Labradoodle with another type of Labradoodle. Others cross them back to purebred poodles. As a result, the mix of poodle and Labrador is not the same in all Labradoodles. Furthermore, the Australian Labradoodle has some cocker spaniel in its bloodlines.

The Labrador retriever shown here was one of the two foundation breeds for the Labradoodle.

The American Labradoodles are crosses strictly between Labs and poodles. However, they are not necessarily half Lab and half poodle.

Looks

Labradoodles come in several sizes, described as miniature, medium, and standard. The smallest Labradoodles are the result of bringing small poodle breeds into the mix.

Smaller breeds of poodles were added to some Labradoodle bloodlines to reduce the dog's size.

The typical Labradoodle's tight, curly hair looks much more like a poodle's than a Labrador's.

The typical Labradoodle is a shaggy dog with curly hair about four to six inches (10 to 15 centimeters) long. The dog's muzzle is slightly narrower than a Lab's. At a glance, a Labradoodle looks something like an English sheepdog with a perm.

Labradoodles of the Past

The Labradoodle is one of the so-called designer dogs. It was developed, or designed, for particular purposes.

Australian Wally Conron began to develop the Labradoodle in 1989 by **crossing** Brandy, a Labrador retriever, with Harley, a standard poodle.

The standard poodle is known for its tight curls and lack of shedding.

Labradors make excellent guide dogs.

Conron was trying to achieve two purposes. He wanted a guide dog to help the blind. He also wanted a dog that would shed very little. Many people have allergies to dogs that shed.

Conron knew that the sturdy, even-tempered Lab had proven to be a wonderful guide dog for blind people. He also knew that the big, standard poodle sheds very little and is often **hypoallergenic**.

Many, but not all, Labradoodles are hypoallergenic.

Harley and Brandy had three pups. Conron called them mixed breed dogs, which they were. They attracted little interest at first. Then he **coined** the name Labradoodle. Suddenly, people showed great interest in the Lab-poodle mix.

Labradoodle pups have become popular and expensive in the United States.

Australian breeders of the Labradoodle eventually added cocker spaniel to the mix.

In the years since Conron's litter, dog breeders in Australia have added cocker spaniel to the Labradoodle's bloodline.

The Dog for You?

Labradoodles are good-natured dogs. They are easy to train and very friendly.

About half of all Labradoodles only shed lightly. They can usually live in families with mild allergies. If allergies are a concern, have the dog's hair tested.

A Labradoodle romps with its owner.

Big, bouncy Labradoodles love to run and play outdoors.

Labradoodles need regular grooming so that their long, curly hair does not mat. Labradoodles also need exercise.

Like most dogs, Labradoodles are happiest when they have attention from humans. As one nine-year old Labradoodle owner said, "They are helpful and they can be therapy dogs and make you feel better!"

A good-natured Labradoodle hugs its nine-year old owner.

Labradoodles often have the warm personality of the Lab.

A Note about Dogs

Puppies are cute and cuddly, but only after serious thought should anybody buy one. Puppies, after all, grow up.

A dog will require more than love and patience. It will need healthy food, exercise, grooming, medical care, and a warm, safe place to live.

A dog can be your best friend, but you need to be its best friend, too.

Choosing the right breed for you requires homework. For more information about buying and owning a dog, contact the American Kennel Club or the Canadian Kennel Club.

Glossary

breed (BREED): a particular kind of domestic animal within a larger, closely related group, such as the Labrador retriever within the dog group

breeders (BREED-urz): those who keep adult dogs and raise their pups, especially those who do so regularly and with great care

coined (KOIND): to make up a name or term

crossing (KRAWS-ing): choosing parents of two different breeds or types for the purpose of having their offspring

guide dog (GIDE-dawg); a dog trained to lead blind people

hypoallergenic (HYE-poh-AL-ur-jen-ik): that which does not cause or is unlikely to cause allergies or an allergic reaction

purebred (PYOOR-bred): an animal of a certain breed with many ancestors of the same breed

temperament (TEM-pur-uh-muhnt): how an animal behaves, such as being even-tempered or hot-tempered

therapy (THER-uh-pee): the help that is offered for a condition or disease

Index

allergies   14, 18

American Labradoodle   10

breed   6, 8

Conron, Wally   13, 14, 15,
   16, 17

designer dogs   13

guide dog   5, 14, 15

Labrador retriever   5, 9,
   10, 14, 16, 20

mixed breed dog   16

poodle   5, 9, 10, 11, 13,
   15, 16

purebred   6, 8

therapy dog   5, 6

cocker spaniel   9, 17

Further Reading

Babineau, Mirriam Fields. *Labradoodles: A Complete Owner's Guide.*
   Kennel Club Books, 2006.
Bonham, Margaret. *Labradoodles*. Barron's Educational Series, 2007.
Wheeler, Jill. *Labradoodles*. ABDO Publishing, 2008.

Website to Visit

www.laa.org.au
www.ilainc.com/index.html

About the Author

Lynn M. Stone is a widely-published wildlife and domestic animal photographer and the author of more than 500 children's books. His book *Box Turtles* was chosen as an Outstanding Science Trade Book and Selectors' Choice for 2008 by the Science Committee of the National Science Teachers' Association and the Children's Book Council.